"Wonderfully narrated and beautifully illustrated, The One O'clock Miracle is a compelling retelling of a famous Bible story of faith, grace and big, powerful words."

DAI HANKEY, author of the "*Eric says...*" series

"Catalina Echeverri's bright, winsome illustrations, combined with texts that faithfully retell both individual Bible stories and God's big story, make for a winning series of picture books."

BOB HARTMAN, author of "*The Prisoners, the Earthquake, and the Midnight Song*" and "*The Bible App for Kids*"

"What a great book for Kids (and for the adults who read it to Kids)! Alison has captured the journey of the anxious father, desperate to find Jesus for his dying son. The story turns on the words of Jesus, "GO your son will live!" Alison's use of repetition in her story and Catalina's beautiful illustrations work together to capture the heart of this story from John 4."

SANDY GALEA, Kidwise Director, Fellowship Dubai

thegoodbook
for children

The One O'Clock Miracle
© Catalina Echeverri / The Good Book Company 2015.
Reprinted 2016, 2017, 2018 (twice), 2019, 2020 (twice), 2021, 2022, 2023.

Illustrated by Catalina Echeverri | Design & Art Direction by André Parker

"The Good Book For Children" is an imprint of The Good Book Company Ltd

thegoodbook.co.uk | thegoodbook.com | thegoodbook.com.au | thegoodbook.co.nz | thegoodbook.co.in

ISBN: 9781910307434 | JOB-007350 | Printed in India

THE ONE O' CLOCK

WRITTEN BY:
Alison Mitchell

and ILLUSTRATED BY:
Catalina Echeverri

MIRACLE

A <u>TRUE</u> STORY ABOUT TRUSTING THE WORDS of JESUS

Long, long ago there lived an important
man who worked for the King.
He was sad and so, so worried.

His son was very ill — so ill
he was going to die...
and no one could help him.

But then...

He heard that a man named Jesus was doing the most amazing, wonderful things.

He heard that Jesus was making ill people well again.

He heard that Jesus was doing things only God can do.

So the man decided to ask Jesus for help.

The man and his son lived
in Capernaum, by the sea.

CAPERNAUM

Sea
of
Galilee

CANA

But Jesus was staying
in Cana, more than
twenty miles away!

It was a very long walk
– and uphill all the way!

But the man had decided that
he MUST see Jesus.

So he said goodbye to
his son and his family, and
he set off to see Jesus.

Up the hill, he walked and walked — and sometimes ran — because he wanted so badly to see Jesus.

The sun went down.
The night was dark and
the stars were bright.
But the man didn't stop.

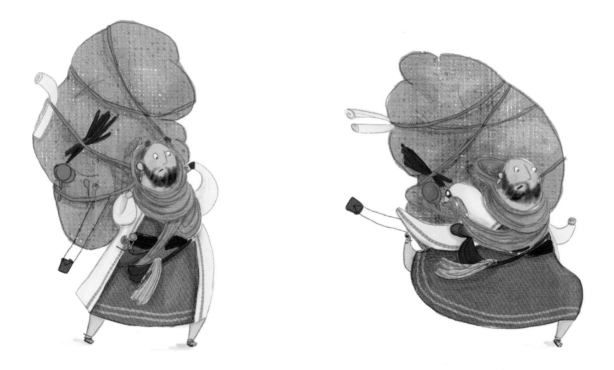

Huffing and puffing, he walked and walked —
and sometimes ran — hurrying to see Jesus.

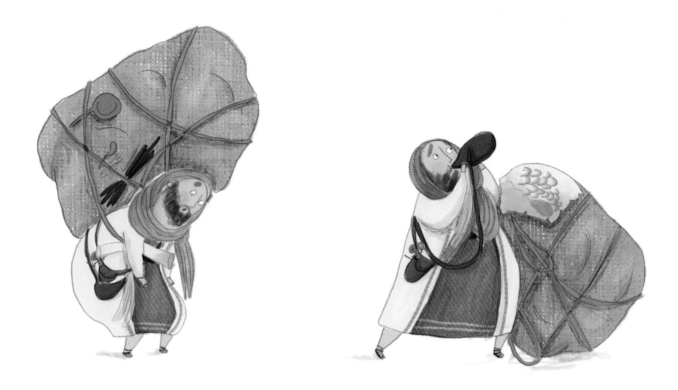

The sun came up.
The morning arrived...

but there was still
a long, long way to go.

Puffing and panting, the man walked and walked — and sometimes ran —

because he **NEEDED** to see Jesus.

At last, at one o'clock in the afternoon, the man reached Cana, the town where Jesus was.

WELCOME TO CANA

He had walked and walked — and sometimes run — and now, at last, he could see Jesus.

"Please, sir," he said. "My son is dying.
Please come with me. Please make him better."
The man knew that if Jesus came with him, and
touched his son, the boy would be well again.

But Jesus just said...

WHAAAT?!

GO HOME...

WITHOUT JESUS?

After all that walking — and even running — to get Jesus to come?!

But Jesus hadn't finished...

"Go," Jesus said.
And then he added:

The man **BELIEVED** him.

Jesus wasn't going to come to the
man's home. He wasn't going to touch
the boy to make him well.

But the man still TRUSTED
that what Jesus said was true.

Down the hill, he walked and walked – and
sometimes ran – because he BELIEVED Jesus.

The sun went down.

The night was dark and the
moon shone brightly.
The man felt so, so tired...

But on and on he walked and
walked — and sometimes ran —
because he TRUSTED Jesus.

LIVE

The sun came up. A new morning arrived and still he walked and walked,

CRACK!!

though his back ached and his legs were very tired.

CANA 10000

CAPERNAUM 5005

YOUR SON WILL LIVE

On he walked and walked —
and sometimes ran — because
he was sure Jesus would
make his son well.

Then, far away in the distance,
he saw some men.

They came closer...

and **CLOSER**...

They were his own servants.

They must have news, he
thought — but what would it be?

"Sir," they said. "It's your son..."

"He is **ALIVE!** He is **WELL AGAIN!**"

The man was bursting for joy.

"**WHEN?**" the man asked.
"When did he get better?"

"Yesterday. At
ONE O'CLOCK
in the afternoon."

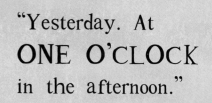

"One o'clock?"
"ONE O'CLOCK!"
the men replied.

Then the man
remembered...

It was ONE O'CLOCK
when he saw Jesus.
It was ONE O'CLOCK
when Jesus said his son would live.
And it was ONE O'CLOCK
when his son got better.

Jesus didn't need to go
and see the boy.
He didn't need to walk
and walk.
He didn't have to run...

JESUS

simply...

SP

OKE

– and just like that, the boy was better.
WOW! Only Jesus could do that!

And do you know why? Because JESUS IS GOD'S SON!

Happy and smiling, the man walked home —
and sometimes he ran — to see his son again.
Then he told his son and his family about
Jesus — and how Jesus could do things only
God can do.

And they all believed in Jesus, God's Son, too.

And now that the man's son was well,
                   what could he do?

He could smile and he could laugh,
he could walk and he could run,
and all because of JESUS!

HOW DO WE KNOW
ABOUT THE ONE O'CLOCK MIRACLE?

The account of Jesus healing the royal official's son was written down for us by John (one of Jesus' friends) in the New Testament part of the Bible.

You will find it in John 4 v 46-54.

It's one of seven miracles that John writes about. At the end of his book, John tells us that the miracles are like signposts pointing to Jesus. They show us who Jesus is—that he is the Son of God, and God's promised Rescuer King (the Christ).

You can read this in John 20 v 30-31.

TALES that Tell the TRUTH

Enjoy all of the award-winning "Tales That Tell The Truth" series:

www.thegoodbook.com | .co.uk